W. F. and J. N. G. RITCHIE

CELTIC WARRIORS

D1115094

SHIRE ARCHAEOLOGY

Cover photograph
An actor portraying a Celtic warrior.
(James Dyer.)

Stuart
tibi lepidum nostrum libellum donamus.

British Library Cataloguing in Publication Data
Ritchie, W. F.
Celtic warriors.——(Shire archaeology; 41)
1.Celts——History   2.Arms and armor, Ancient——
Great Britain   3.Arms and armor, Ancient——France.
I. Title II. Ritchie, Graham
623.4'41'094   U805

ISBN 0-85263-714-4

Published by
SHIRE PUBLICATIONS LTD
Cromwell House, Church Street, Princes Risborough,
Aylesbury, Bucks HP17 9AJ, UK.

Series Editor: James Dyer

ISBN 085263 714 4

First published 1985

Set in 11 point Times and printed in Great Britain by
C. I. Thomas & Sons (Haverfordwest) Ltd.
Press Buildings, Merlins Bridge, Haverfordwest, Dyfed.

Contents

4

List of illustrations

Preface and acknowledgements

This volume stems from the notion that a greater knowledge about the continental Celtic tribes could usefully be made available as an adjunct to classical and archaeological studies by illustrating the exciting range of archaeological material available. The various references to the Celtic tribes and their customs might also be studied, on the one hand as linguistic texts and on the other hand (in translation perhaps) as historical documents. For the idea that the Romans were confronted by 'barbarian tribes' makes it difficult to examine dispassionately the cultural collision that was such an important event in western Europe in the later first millennium BC.

We are grateful to the many museums and libraries which have offered every assistance as our independent examinations of the two types of evidence have progressed. We are grateful to Professor Stuart Piggott for his valued support over many years; Professor D. W. Harding read the text and made a number of useful suggestions. The assistance of Dr D. J. Breeze, Dr P. D. C. Brown, Dr D. V. Clarke, Dr John Collis, Miss Felicity Kinross, Dr I. H. Longworth, Dr Anna Ritchie and Dr M. Rusu is gratefully acknowledged. The help of Mrs E. Glass and Mr I. G. Scott has improved the finished volume immeasurably.

We are grateful in particular to the following institutions and friends for permission to reproduce illustrations: Ashmolean Museum, with the kind assistance of Dr P. D. C. Brown, figs. 2, 24; *Birmingham Post and Mail,* fig. 18; the BBC, with the kind permission of Mr Robin Fairweather and the generous assistance of Miss Felicity Kinross, figs. 5, 13-15; British Museum, figs. 19, 22-24, 28; C. Boube-Piccot, fig. 6; City of Kingston upon Hull Museums and Art Galleries, fig. 8; National Museum of Antiquities of Scotland, Edinburgh, figs. 10, 20, 24-5; National Museum of Denmark, Copenhagen, fig. 11; National Museum of Ireland, Dublin, fig. 21; National Museum of Switzerland, Zurich, fig. 29; Dr Mircea Rusu, Cluj, figs. 26 and 30; Mr I. G. Scott, figs. 1, 9, 12, 16-17, 27.

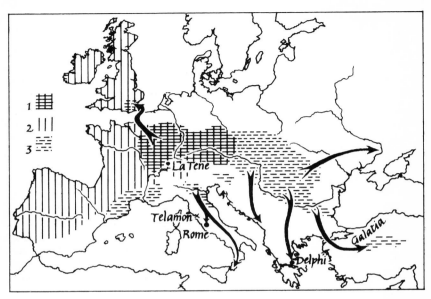

Fig. 1. Europe showing the main areas of Celtic influence: 1, the heartland of the Celtic world; 2, Celtic expansion in prehistoric times; 3, additional Celtic settlement in historical times.

1
Who were the Celts?

The people known to archaeologists as Celts lived to the north of the Alps in what is now southern Germany and eastern France from about 500 BC (fig. 1). They spoke a language which was ancestral to the Celtic languages of today—Breton, Gaelic, Irish and Welsh. According to the Greek writer Ephorus, the Celts were one of the four great barbarian peoples, the others being the Persians, the Scythians and the Lybians. Celtic society comprised a number of tribes which were never fused into a unified nation, but the names of many of the tribes have come down to us through the writings of Greek and Roman authors. As a people the Celts were called *Keltai* (or *Keltoi*) and *Galatai* by the Greeks, and *Celtae, Galli* and *Galatae* by the Romans, though we cannot be sure by what name they described themselves. They were a mobile folk, raiding and in some cases settling far from home. Various reasons are given for these migrations, which began about 400 BC—overpopulation, search for a better climate or, as they were warriors, a delight in war and booty. At the height of their expansion Celts were to be found in the Iberian peninsula, in Gaul and northern Italy, down the Danube valley, through Greece and across the Hellespont to Galatia in Asia Minor. From 369 BC they served as mercenaries to local rulers in Greece, Asia Minor and Egypt. They also enlisted in the invading armies of the Carthaginians and served under Roman commanders in Italy, Asia Minor and north Africa.

In many areas the archaeological evidence shows that the Celts enjoyed a common material culture, and this can be particularly well illustrated by one segment of Celtic society—the warriors. The Celts as farmers, craftsmen and architects—for the planning and execution of a large hillfort is comparable in scale to the building of a cathedral—are beyond the scope of this volume. Celtic society embraced several main classes: in the upper tier were the aristocrats, the noble wealthy families, from which the rulers would be drawn as well as the leaders of warrior bands, druids and bards. In the next group were the farmers and craftsmen, and below them were the unfree workers and the slaves, though slavery did not play a large role.

Celtic people became important in several parts of Europe after moving from their Rhineland centres. These great movements were responsible for the establishment of Celtic society in northern Italy from 400 BC until their defeat by the Romans at the battle of Telamon in 225 BC. With the expansion of Roman power first in Italy and then over much of western Europe and Asia Minor, Celtic ways of life were largely subjugated to Roman authority, surviving only in areas peripheral to the original centres. Later Celtic society and traditions, in Ireland particularly, have been shown to mirror many features of the Celtic tribes of prehistory.

These movements of people need not be the only explanation for the adoption of Celtic language and customs in other areas. In Britain, for example, there is no evidence for large-scale migrations to account for those facets of life that take on a 'Celtic' aspect in the second half of the first millennium BC. The underlying continuity in building traditions and material culture shows that there were no sudden or radical changes in everyday life. Society became 'Celtic' by a form of cultural osmosis— something that is impossible to document from the archaeological record. The vision of the wagon train of the American western film is much more understandable as a mechanism for culture change. From a Celtic standpoint such movements were indeed known, in, for example, the migration of the Helvetii in 58 BC, which is described by Caesar; but no seaborne flotilla can be invoked for the adoption of Celtic ways in Britain, except for the Belgae in the early first century BC.

'Barbarians' used to have a bad reputation; the civilising influence of the Mediterranean world, so crucial to the development of European literary and artistic achievements, has perhaps coloured our view of peoples beyond the frontiers of the Greek and Roman world, peoples with different social traditions or ways of life. Today one of the most popular and vociferous protagonists of barbarian freedom is a shrewd, cunning little warrior, to whom all perilous missions are immediately entrusted—Asterix, the creation of Goscinny and Uderzo. A parallel may be drawn between the characterisation of the Gauls of the Asterix tales and the presentation of warriors in classical writings. The chief of Asterix's tribe, Vitalstatistix, is majestic, brave, hot-tempered and red-headed—the stereotype for a Celtic chieftain. Classical authors also tended to perpetuate the idea of 'national types'. Several of the descriptions given in the pages of this volume may equally evoke more what Greek or Roman audiences expected to hear rather than observed 'fact'.

Fig. 2. Terracotta figurine of a barbarian warrior with distinctively Celtic hairstyle, moustache and shield with midrib and central strip boss.

Our knowledge of the Celts and their world comes on the whole from such writers as Polybius, Diodorus Siculus, Pausanias, Strabo and Dio Cassius (all of whom wrote in Greek) and from Caesar, Livy and Tacitus among the Roman historians. Short, passing references in the works of Herodotus, Xenophon, Plato and Aristotle show that the Celts were known as a 'national type' quite early. The earlier writers give a romantic picture of the Celts with a greater stress on such aspects as single combat and their wearing of neck ornaments; Caesar and Tacitus are more matter of fact. It must always be remembered that we are dealing with evidence about 'barbarian' peoples from authors of several different periods, who were predominantly pro-Roman, ready to justify the Roman way of life and government, and who were often ignorant of details of the Celtic world, and some of whom were uncritical of their sources. Because something was written down twenty centuries ago, it is not necessarily true. One example of the lack of detail is shown in the Roman unconcern about the barbarian Celts—very seldom is the name of the chieftain recorded. But they do report that Brennus led the attack on Rome in 390 BC, and that Britomartus fought against Marcellus at Clastidium in 222 BC. Caesar is more knowledgeable, indeed he served for eight years in Gaul, and he gives the names of Gallic leaders, Vercingetorix and others; Tacitus names the Caledonian leader, Calgacus, at the battle of Mons Graupius in AD 84 and provides him with a suitably rousing battle oration. The Celts, however, have left no written record themselves, at least in part because of their custom of oral transmission of law, tradition and religious practices, with the result that we lack the equivalent of Asterix's side of the story, and archaeology is but a partial replacement.

There are also tangible representations of idealised Celts, as the terracotta figures of Graeco-Roman origin show; fig. 2 illustrates a moustachioed barbarian with flowing locks, short tunic, trousers, a sword and an oval shield. A finer piece of artistic expression, this time of the Celt in defeat, is the 'Dying Gaul' (fig 3), a naked warrior with distinctive hairstyle and a characteristic neck ornament or torc. With the rise of nationalism in the mid to late nineteenth century, a new awareness of the Celtic past of northern Europe prompted such proud statues as that of Ambiorix, king of the Eburones (fig 4), whose style finds echoes in the costumes of Asterix today. If each age evokes its own reaction to barbarians, the contemporary warrior made up for the BBC schools television series *Out of the Past* is the most

Fig. 3 *(above left)*. The 'Dying Gaul'; detail of the head and torso of a marble copy of a statue set up at Pergamon in Asia Minor; the torc and hairstyle are carefully modelled.

Fig. 4 *(above right)*. Ambiorix, king of the Eburones; a nineteenth-century view of a Celtic chieftain at Tongern, Belgium.

Fig. 5 *(right)*. A Celtic warrior: an actor is made up for his part in a BBC schools *Out of the Past* television programme.

archaeologically accurate (fig 5).

Language, which plays such an important part in our identification of a Celtic tradition, is scarcely mentioned by classical writers. Momigliano has put the problem succinctly: 'Ancient ethnography gives little space to language. Comparative philology had not been invented. Ethnic groups were defined in terms of common descent and of common institutions.' In a similar way the archaeological approach, for example linking warrior burials over a wide geographical area, seeks to illustrate common institutions with the material evidence at its disposal. Any study of the Celtic warrior thus depends both on an evaluation of the literary evidence, often from authors unsympathetic to the Celtic way of life, and on a discussion of the archaeological evidence, itself frequently patchy. First, however, we shall examine the general impressions that Greek and Roman authors provided for their contemporary readers.

2
The Celts through Greek and Roman eyes

Physical appearance

To the Greeks and Romans the Celts presented a terrifying sight because of their tall stature and their strange appearance. They were in many respects different from Mediterranean peoples. The Celts were by far the tallest race in the world, noticeable also for their white skin and fair hair.

Although the Greeks and Romans had heard about the barbarian Celts, they first encountered them as warriors, and it was in battle that their enormous size and strange appearance first struck them. The Celtic chiefs who advanced to challenge their opposing Roman leader to single combat were men of great physique, 'of stature greater than human'; the story of the fight between Britomartus and Marcellus can be compared to that between Goliath and David. The triumphal procession awarded to Marcellus was said to be most remarkable for the riches of the spoils and the gigantic size of the prisoners.

Diodorus Siculus describes the Celts at some length: 'the Gauls are tall of body, with skin moist and white; their hair is blond not only by nature but also because they practise to increase artificially the peculiar nature of their colouring. Some of them shave off their beards but others let them grow moderately: the nobles shave their cheeks but let their moustaches grow freely so as to cover their mouths. Therefore, when they are eating, the moustaches become mixed in the food, and when they are drinking, the drink passes as if through a strainer.'

They had unusual styles of hairdressing; they used to smear their hair with limewater and then pull it back to the top of their head and over the neck to produce something like a horse's mane (an attempt to illustrate this is shown in fig. 2). Tacitus tells of other similar treatments of hair found among the Germanic tribes. Thus the Suebi are distinguished from the other Germans by their particular hairstyle: 'they comb their hair sideways and tie it in a knot . . . often on the very crown.' All this elaborate hairdressing was intended to give them greater height and to terrify their enemies in battle. Silius Italicus mentions a warrior who had offered his golden locks and the ruddy top-knot on the crown of his head to Mars if he were victorious.

The colour of the hair is usually referred to as fair, red or flaxen-coloured and even ginger. The men of Britain were taller than those of Gaul, but their hair was not so fair, while the Germans differed only slightly from other Celts in that they were wilder, taller and had redder hair. There is a story that Caligula, anxious to make his triumph in Rome more spectacular, in view of the small number of prisoners for display, picked out some very tall Gauls and made them not only grow their hair longer but also dye it red.

Strabo, quoting an earlier source, makes a curious statement: 'they try to avoid becoming stout and pot-bellied and any young man whose waist exceeds the measure of the normal girdle is fined.' But such a weight-watching approach is contradicted by other writers who tell of the Gauls gorging themselves with food and drinking wine excessively so that their bodies soon become corpulent and flabby. Consequently, when they exercised their bodies, they suffered quickly from exhaustion and breathlessness.

In the minds of classical writers the women were not only like their men in stature, but they could also rival them in strength. Ammianus Marcellinus described how difficult it would be for a band of foreigners to deal with a Celt if he called in the help of his wife. For she was stronger than he was and could rain blows and kicks upon the assailants equal in force to the shots of a catapult. Boudica, queen of the Iceni, was said to be 'very tall and terrifying in appearance; her voice was very harsh and a great mass of red hair fell over her shoulders.'

Dress and ornaments

According to Diodorus Siculus, the Celts 'wear striking clothing, tunics dyed and embroidered in many colours, and trousers which they call *bracae:* and they wear striped cloaks, fastened by a brooch, thick in winter and light in summer, worked in a variegated, closely set check pattern.' Strabo says that instead of the ordinary tunics they wore 'split tunics which have sleeves and reach down to their thighs. Their wool is rough and thin at the ends and from it they weave thick cloaks (*sagi*) which they call *laenae.*' The poet Propertius tells how the huge Celtic chief Virdomarus, skilled in hurling his javelins from his chariot and 'clothed in striped trousers', boasted of his descent from the Rhine God.

Three pieces of clothing are thus mentioned: trousers, tunics and cloaks. The trousers would certainly be noticed by the toga-wearing Romans. Trousers were worn especially by the

Fig. 6. A fragment of a monumental bronze statue from Volubilis, Morocco, probably showing a captive Briton with trousers with a check pattern.

cavalrymen, and the Romans themselves adopted them from the mercenary Gallic cavalry they enlisted. The tunic was probably a simple garment like a shirt, made of linen and reaching down to the thighs. There was also the slightly different style mentioned by Strabo—with slits and sleeves. The Iberians were said to wear short tunics bordered with a purple stripe and dazzlingly white. The tunics were often dyed and embroidered and worn with a gold-plated or silver-plated belt. The cloaks were made of wool; they were heavy or light according to the season and were fastened at the shoulder by a brooch. A defeated Celtic barbarian is shown on a fragment of a monumental bronze statue from Volubilis in Roman Mauretania in north Africa; his *bracae* have what Piggott has described as 'loud and disparate check patterns' (fig. 6) and his cloak hangs loosely from his shoulders. Such an impression of woven designs is also given in a description of

Queen Boudica, who wore a tunic of many colours over which a thick cloak was fastened by a brooch.

An outstanding characteristic of the Celtic people was their love of decoration and ornament. 'They collect a great quantity of gold and use it for decoration, not only the women but also the men. For they wear bracelets on the wrists and arms, necklaces of solid gold, rings of great worth and even gold corslets' (body armour for the upper part of the torso). The torc was one of the most important ornaments worn by the Celts. It was a neck ring made of a rod of metal (sometimes twisted), of bronze or gold according to the wealth and status of the wearer. The two ends of the torc almost met, but the metal was pliant, for it had to open sufficiently to let it on or off (figs. 3 and 5). The torc of the Gallic chief slain by Titus Manlius was rich and attractive enough for him to take as the only trophy of the combat, and thus he gained the name *Torquatus*. Torcs formed part of the booty paraded in triumphs by Roman generals. They are listed along with the military standards taken, and they must have been considered a very precious and important object, because the Gauls gave one to Augustus, 'a golden necklet a hundred pounds in weight'. Bracelets, armlets, rings and brooches were the other main pieces of decoration. A replica of the torc from Snettisham (Norfolk) is shown on the neck of the warrior in fig. 5 and a plainer torc on fig. 3. As with clothes, so with adornments, each man wore what he could afford and what his status demanded. It is obvious, however, that the Celts liked to attract attention with flamboyant clothes and rich, decorative accessories. The Roman soldiers were well aware of the splendid ornaments worn by their opponents and before one battle they were told by their generals that soldiers should not be adorned with gold and silver but should rely on their weapons and their courage. These ornaments were more truly booty than arms, shining brightly before the battle but ugly in the midst of blood and wounds.

Food

Athenaeus is the main authority on food; quoting Posidonius, he says: 'Their food consists of a small quantity of bread and a large amount of meat'; and quoting Phylarchus, 'Many loaves of bread are broken up and served lavishly on tables as well as pieces of meat taken from cauldrons.' Bread, meat (boiled in a cauldron or roasted on a spit) and fish were the staple foods. Fish was eaten, 'sometimes baked with salt, vinegar and cummin'. By contrast the Caledonians and the Maeatae, according to Dio, never ate fish, though it was in plentiful supply. Strabo speaks of large quantities of food, milk and all kinds of meat, especially fresh and salted pork, and of the Britons, who, though they had milk in abundance, did not make cheese.

A certain etiquette and precedence were observed at table, and good eating habits were even noted. Though they were accustomed to eat voraciously, raising up whole limbs in both hands and biting off the meat, they did it in a cleanly fashion. No one started to eat without looking first to see if the chief had touched what was set before him. In extending hospitality to strangers they did not ask them who they were and what they wanted until they had eaten.

At more formal gatherings or celebrations they sat in a circle with the chief or hero in the centre, his attendants and warriors around and behind him, each with a position according to his status. Drink was served from earthenware or bronze jugs and the meat on plates of bronze or in baskets. When the joints of meat were served, the chief or hero took the thigh piece. But if someone else claimed it, they joined in single combat to the death. Frequently they used some chance circumstance to start an argument and then a fight during dinner. They indulged in sham fights and practice feints and they would end up either wounding or even killing their opponent. This love of quarrelling and fighting even at table was made all the easier, says Polybius, because they usually ate too much and drank too much.

The Celtic chiefs were accompanied in war and in peace by 'parasites' (the word means fellow diner and has no pejorative meaning), who sang their praises before the assembly; these entertainers were called bards.

There are also descriptions of great banquets prepared by rich kings. The gestures of lordly prodigality and ostentation were typical of the autocratic tribal chief of the period. Louernius, king of the Arverni, in an attempt to win favour, is said to have ridden his chariot over a plain distributing gold and silver to all who followed him. He also gave a feast to all who wished to attend, in a vast enclosure, the sides of which were 1½ miles (2.4 km) long. He filled vats with liquor, prepared great quantities of food and ensured service without interruption for several days. A poet who arrived too late for the festivities composed a poem praising the king's greatness and lamenting the fact he had arrived too late. So charmed was the king by the song that he gave the poet a purse of gold and won for himself a further poetic effusion.

Wine

One feature which has attracted frequent comment was the ability of the Celts to drink great quantities of liquor, though one should not take Plutarch seriously when he says that the Celts were so enthralled by the new pleasure of wine drinking that they seized their arms, took their families and set off for Italy! Athenaeus says: 'the drink of the wealthy is wine imported from Italy . . . This is unmixed, but sometimes a little water is added. The lower classes drink a beer made from wheat and prepared with honey . . . They drink from a common cup, a little at a time, not more than a mouthful, but they do it rather frequently.' The Cimbri were said to be demoralised by the delights of wine, but the Nervii, a Gallic tribe famed for their indomitable ferocity, would not allow wine and other luxuries to be imported because they believed that with them the men would become too soft and effeminate to endure hardship.

Celtic character

To Polybius the Celts were merely a band of marauders who later became mercenaries ready to join whichever side suited them in the war between the Romans and the Carthaginians. They were brave and ostentatiously courageous but reckless, impetuous and easily disheartened. Hannibal was eager to make use of their enthusiasm before it wore off; but the Carthaginians and the Romans too were apprehensive of the Celts, for they saw in them a lack of fidelity and a mutual treachery. It is reported that Hannibal so distrusted his new allies that he had a number of wigs made for himself, suitable for men of all ages. He was sure that by changing his wigs constantly he would make it difficult for the fickle Celts to recognise and perhaps kill him.

Some writers tend to dwell mainly on their lawlessness and savagery. Cicero, for example, makes great use of this to rail against them. 'They thought it right to sacrifice human beings to the immortal gods' and 'they find it necessary to propitiate the immortal gods and to defile their altars and temples with human victims.' Polybius and Livy concentrate on the outrages committed by the Gauls and on the barbarous character of the Galatians. There was always a tendency for Greek or Roman writers to emphasise characteristics which did not conform to their code of morality and perhaps give too much credence to the more dramatic traveller's tales. Strabo and Diodorus Siculus, while not ignoring the savagery of some Celtic practices, also describe some of the more pleasing traits of their character.

3
Warrior burials

In common with many early societies, the dead were buried in full clothing, perhaps in some cases clad in especially fine ceremonial garments and accoutrements. The clothes rarely survive, although occasionally impressions and even fragments of textiles are preserved on metal objects by the processes of corrosion; the jewellery and metal fastenings, particularly those made of bronze and iron, remain in the graves for archaeologists to excavate and record. Weapons and even food and drink were also buried, and the graves can thus tell us much about how the warrior was dressed, armed and provisioned at various stages in Celtic history.

One of the most complete warrior burials was discovered at La Gorge Meillet in the Marne department of France in 1876; a pit measuring about 3.2 metres (10 feet 6 inches) by 2.4 metres (7 feet 10½ inches) and up to 1.7 metres (5 feet 7 inches) deep had been dug into the chalk subsoil. A two-wheeled chariot with rich fittings had been buried (fig. 7) with the body of the warrior laid out on its platform and his weapons displayed on the floor of the grave. None of the wooden or wicker parts of the chariot survived but the layout of the bronze and iron components gives us a reasonable impression of its size. The wheels were set in specially dug slots in the floor of the grave pit and we thus know that they were about 1.3 metres (4 feet 3 inches) apart; the iron tyres show that the wheels were just under 1 metre (3 feet 3 inches) in diameter. The axle had bronze bands and elaborately decorated hub caps. The burial was not that of a gnarled warrior but of a comparatively young person; he had a gold bracelet on his left arm and was accompanied by a long iron sword, four spears with iron blades and butts to their shafts, and an elaborate bronze helmet. All that remained to indicate his clothing was a bronze brooch and on his chest four bronze buttons decorated with rosettes, with the fragmentary remains of his worsted tunic still traceable. Horse harness was represented by the two bronze bits and by chains with attractive terminals inlaid with coral. At the foot of the burial a platter of rough grey pottery contained joints of pork, fowl and eggs, accompanied by an iron knife with an elaborate handle with a bronze knob. There were two other pottery vessels including a tall pedestalled urn made on a potter's wheel. A magnificent bronze wine flagon is one of the most significant grave goods, for it is not of Celtic but of Etruscan manufacture. In the upper part of the grave pit there was a second burial, inserted in the course of the filling of the shaft, a mature male accompanied by a sword and by an iron ring that was doubtless part of the fittings of his sword belt.

The Etruscan flagon illustrates the Celtic delight, noted by classical authors, in wine imported from the Mediterranean, and it also indicates that the date of the burial at La Gorge Meillet was about 450 BC. The known sequences of metalwork and pottery from certain Mediterranean sources provide good dating evidence for burials (despite reservations about the possibility that some objects at least might have been heirlooms when they were deposited). At Somme Bionne, also in the Marne, a chariot burial was accompanied by weapons, a wine flagon and a Greek pottery vessel dating to about 420 BC. The warrior had also been provided with joints of wild boar, pig and duck, as well as a collection of frogs in a pot! Originally the burial had probably been covered by a large mound, but over the centuries this had been flattened.

Such burials are a valuable source of information about leading Celtic warriors. Long iron swords in decorated scabbards, hung from elaborate sword belts, sheaves of spears and sometimes elaborate, but not very functional, helmets accompanied the burial. Shields were also used, although normally only the metal hand grip survives with early burials; there is, however, much more information about shields in the period after about 350 BC. Standing on their chariots with their richly harnessed horses, the warriors must have been very impressive sights.

From the mid fourth century BC Celtic warriors were buried with their weapons in, for example, France, Germany, Poland and Switzerland. Warrior burials are a less recurrent feature in Britain, though some are known, including a group of chariot burials in Humberside, including Garton Slack (fig. 8). In a most exciting discovery in 1984 two chariot burials were laid bare in the course of gravel digging at Wetwang Slack, a continuation of the Garton Slack quarry, where the outline of an iron tyre alerted the driver of the mechanical excavator; the tyres and hub of the wheel as well as the outline of one of the chariot poles still survived. One burial was that of a woman, the other of a warrior accompanied by a sword in a scabbard, seven spears and fragments of the iron spine of a shield. The evidence from La Gorge Meillet and Garton Slack is used in the reconstruction of the Celtic chariot in chapter 4. In Britain several inhumation

Fig. 7. Chariot burial from La Gorge Meillet, Somme Tourbe (Marne, France), excavated in 1876.

Fig. 8. Chariot burial from Garton Slack (Humberside), excavated in 1971, and now displayed in the Transport and Archaeology Museum, Kingston upon Hull, showing the bridle bits, the harness fittings, the dismantled wheels with iron tyres and the stains of the twelve spokes. Part of the chariot pole, which had been broken in two, survived as a stain and is visible beyond the skeleton.

burials accompanied by weapons have been recorded and that from Owslebury (Hampshire), one of a handful of well excavated examples, is illustrated on fig 9. There are at least two cremation burials where the boss of the accompanying shield survives, Snailwell (Cambridgeshire) and Stanfordbury (Bedfordshire).

We have drawn five extended inhumation burials to approximately the same scale in order to show the main pieces of surviving weaponry (fig. 9). At Connantre, in the Marne, the warrior had two iron brooches at his shoulders, and his body is covered by an oval shield, of which the boss and the iron strip providing additional protection around the edge survive; beside him were an iron sword with the chain by which it hung from his belt and an iron spearhead and butt, and there were three other iron objects of uncertain purpose near his right foot. At Gourgançon (Marne) a more rectilinear shield is suggested by the outline of the binding strip and a rather more elaborate boss has covered the hand grip. From Velká Maňa in Slovakia, part of grave 28 is illustrated; the burial was accompanied by a sword, spear and shield, the rim of which survived to give the impression of a truly man-sized shield. At Kietrz in southern Poland a sword and spear were laid out on the right side of the body with a pottery vessel on the left; there was an iron fibula on the chest.

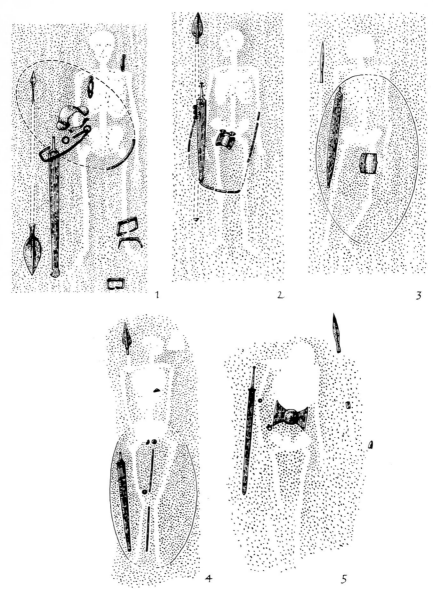

Fig. 9. Celtic warrior burials: extended inhumations. 1, Connantre (Marne, France); 2, Gourgançon (Marne, France); 3, Velká Maňa (Slovakia); 4, Kietrz (southern Poland); 5, Owslebury (Hampshire).

Much of the iron binding of the oval shield remained and also a strengthening strip that had covered the midrib; at least seven round-headed nails appear to have added both decoration and solidity. The burial from Owslebury (Hampshire) was that of a warrior aged between about forty and fifty years. The sword in a wooden scabbard with leather binding was to the right, with spear, ferrule and butt to the left; the shaft of the spear appeared to have been broken in order to get it into the grave. Two rings and a belt hook showed the method by which the sword was hung from the belt. Across the body had lain a wooden shield with a bronze boss and, although the outline of the shield could not be determined, it is possible that it had been made up of three planks of wood about 13 millimetres (½ inch) thick. The boss had a raised central point and had been carefully shaped to provide protection for the hand grip and central spine of the shield, both of which were presumably of wood. The burial belongs to the later first century BC.

A warrior burial was discovered at Whitcombe (Dorset) in 1967; the crouched inhumation in an oval hollow was that of a powerfully built man of about twenty-seven, accompanied by a bronze brooch, an iron spearhead and a splendid sword, which had been buried in a wooden scabbard. The decorated mountings of the scabbard remained as well as two iron suspension rings. The burial is of first century BC date.

A grave at Acklam (North Yorkshire), found in 1980, measuring 1.25 metres (4 feet 1 inch) by 1.1 metres (3 feet 7 inches) and about 0.4 metres (1 foot 4 inches) deep, contained the crouched inhumation of an adult male who appears to have died from severe wounding to the back of the head, possibly with a sword. A sword, bent perhaps as part of the ritual of deposition, was found in the grave. Several burials where spearheads were found embedded in the body, perhaps as a result of battle or punishment, have been found.

In this chapter some of the range of weaponry from Celtic graves has been illustrated because the objects shown were probably in use together on the battlefield, and because the graves contain objects that were, with a few possible exceptions, actually used, rather than being specially made for parade or show.

4
The Celts in battle

Polybius, who lived between about 202 and 120 BC, gives a full account of how the Celts fought at the battle of Telamon in 225 BC; it is worth quoting at length because it highlights several recurring characteristics: 'The Celts had drawn up the Gaesatae from the Alps to face their enemies on the rear ... and behind them the Insubres .... The Insubres and the Boii wore trousers and light cloaks, but the Gaesatae in their overconfidence had thrown these aside and stood in front of the whole army naked, with nothing but their arms; for they thought that thus they would be more efficient, since some of the ground was overgrown with thorns which would catch on their clothes and impede the use of their weapons.

'On the other hand the fine order and the noise of the Celtic host terrified the Romans; for there were countless trumpeters and horn blowers and since the whole army was shouting its war cries at the same time there was such a confused sound that the noise seemed to come not only from the trumpeters and the soldiers but also from the countryside which was joining in the echo. No less terrifying were the appearance and gestures of the naked warriors in front, all of whom were in the prime of life and of excellent physique. All the warriors in the front ranks were adorned with gold torcs and armlets. The Romans were particularly terrified by the sight of these men, but, led on by hope of gain, they were twice as keen to face the danger.

'... to the Celts in the rear their trousers and cloaks afforded good protection, but to the naked men in front events turned out differently to what they had expected and caused them much discomfiture and distress. For since the Gallic shield cannot cover the whole body, because they were naked, the bigger they were, the more chance there was of missiles striking home. At length, unable to ward off the javelin throwers because of the distance and the number of javelins falling upon them, in despair and distress some rushed upon the enemy in wild rage and willingly gave up their lives; others, retreating step by step towards their comrades, threw them into confusion by their manifest show of cowardice.'

The ancient writers dwelt upon the terrifying effect an army of Celts had on their opponents; their great stature, their wild cries, their gesticulations and prancings, the clashing of arms and blowing of trumpets — all combined to terrify and confuse the enemy. As long as these demonstrations of enthusiasm and bravado struck terror into the foe, the Celts would drive all before them. 'For they were always most formidable while they were fresh.' The whole race is war-mad, says Strabo, high-spirited and quick to fight, but otherwise straightforward and not at all of evil character.

Single combat

When the two armies were arrayed in line, the loud voice of the Celtic chief could sometimes be heard. 'For they were accustomed ... to come forward before the front line and challenge the bravest of the enemy drawn up opposite them to single combat, brandishing their weapons and terrifying the enemy. Whenever one accepts the challenge, they praise in song the manly virtues of their ancestors, proclaiming also their own brave deeds. At the same time they abuse and belittle their opponent, trying by their words to rob him of his boldness of spirit beforehand.'

The story of how Marcus Claudius Marcellus killed a Gallic leader at Clastidium (222 BC) is typical of such encounters. Advancing with a smallish army, Marcellus met a combined force of Insubrian Gauls and Gaesatae at Clastidium. The Gallic army advanced with the usual rush and terrifying cries, and their king, Britomartus, picking out Marcellus by means of his badges of rank, made for him, shouting a challenge and brandishing his spear. Britomartus was an outstanding figure not only for his size but also for his adornments; for he was resplendent in bright colours and his armour shone with gold and silver. This armour, thought Marcellus, would be a fitting offering to the gods. He charged the Gaul, pierced his bright breastplate and cast him to the ground. It was an easy task to kill Britomartus and strip him of his armour. These spoils Marcellus offered to Jupiter. This is the only story of its kind in which the name of the Celtic chief is recorded.

Noise

In their attempts to throw the enemy into confusion and terror, the Celts made great use of noise. They yelled their war cries as they advanced, howling and singing and brandishing their spears. Livy, in two different contexts, distant in time and place, vividly depicts the noise accompanying their mad rush into battle. Describing the battle of the river Allia, he says: 'they are given to wild outbursts and they fill the air with hideous songs and varied

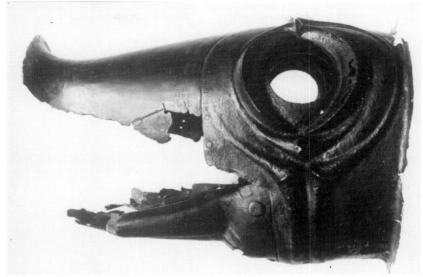

Fig. 10. The mouth of a Celtic trumpet from Deskford (Banffshire, Grampian), wrought in sheet bronze.

shouts.' Of the Gauls in Asia he writes: 'their songs as they go into battle, their yells and leapings, and the dreadful noise of arms as they beat their shields in some ancestral custom — all this is done with one purpose, to terrify their enemies.' In sharp contrast to the wild onset of the Celts, which was evident also during their invasion of Greece, was the silent, orderly advance of the Greek army. When the Gauls defeated the Roman army at the river Allia, they marched on Rome. 'They arrived at the city and entered at first in fear lest there should be some treachery, but then, when they saw that the city was deserted, they moved forward with equal noise and impetuosity.' On another occasion the Romans experienced a new form of noisy warfare: 'for standing up in chariots and wagons, the armed enemies came at them with the great noise of hooves and wheels so that the unfamiliar din terrified the horses of the Romans.'

There was also the noise of trumpets. At the battle of Telamon the number of trumpeters and horn blowers was incalculable. Diodorus Siculus says they had trumpets peculiar to barbarians: 'for when they blow upon them, they produce a harsh sound, suitable to the tumult of war.' The Gauls also had their shouts of victory and triumph. 'They shouted "Victory, Victory" in their

Fig. 11. The Gundestrup Cauldron, from Denmark, showing trumpeters, footsoldiers with spears and shields, a soldier with a sword and helmet surmounted by a boar, and two cavalrymen wearing spurs and helmets surmounted by a boar and a bird.

customary fashion and raised their yell of triumph (*ululatus*)', and at Alesia 'they encouraged their men with shouts of triumph (*clamore et ululatu*)'. There are several representations of Celtic trumpets on classical sculpture, most notably at Pergamon in Asia Minor, and on the triumphal arch at Orange in southern France, and a few fragments of actual trumpets have survived.

The mouth of a trumpet shaped in the manner of a boar's head was found in 1816 at Deskford (Banffshire, Grampian), (fig. 10); although the trumpet itself no longer survives, the mouth may be compared with the representations on the cauldron from Gundestrup in Denmark, where the sectional nature of the trumpet construction is clearly shown (fig. 11). The Deskford trumpet may originally have had ears and a mane rather like the Gundestrup examples; when first discovered, however, it retained a movable wooden 'tongue' which may have added vibration to the strident sounds blown from it. The Deskford piece is usually dated to the middle of the first century AD.

Among the earlier representations of trumpets are those from the temple of Athena Polias Nikephoros at Pergamon in Asia Minor dating to about 181 BC and celebrating the victories of Attalus I over the Galatian tribes in the late third century BC. Trumpets, shields, standards, indeed all the trophies are set out in a great display of spoils of war on the triumphal arch at Orange (fig. 12). The large number of trumpets shown at Orange underlines the impression of great noise during battle given by the classical writers.

Naked warriors

As already mentioned, Polybius describes a contingent of Gaesatae (sometimes taken as mercenaries, now more often as spearmen), which took part in the battle of Telamon; they came from beyond the Alps to help the Gauls already in north Italy (for example the Boii and the Insubres). The Celts of north Italy wore trousers and cloaks, but the Gaesatae fought naked. At the battle of Cannae (216 BC) Polybius describes the naked Celts and the Iberians with their short linen tunics with purple borders, and Livy speaks of the Gauls naked from the navel up and of the Iberians with dazzlingly white tunics bordered with purple. The Celts in Asia Minor seem to have preserved this custom, for they too are described as naked in battle with skin white because they were never exposed except in battle. Camillus, trying to raise the morale of the Romans after the siege of the Capitol, pointed to some naked Gauls and said: 'These are the men who rush against you in battle, who raise loud shouts, clash their arms and long swords, and toss their hair. Look at their lack of hardiness, their soft and flabby bodies, and go to it'. Dionysus of Halicarnassus expresses the same sentiments: 'Our enemies fight bare-headed, their breasts, sides, thighs, legs are all bare, and they have no protection except from their shields; their weapons of defence are thin spears and long swords. What injury could their long hair,

Fig. 12. Arc de Triomphe, Orange (Vaucluse, France); details of trumpets and standards.

Fig. 13. Celtic chariot with warrior and charioteer; the reconstructed chariot, now in the National Museum of Antiquities of Scotland, Edinburgh, is the result of the amalgamation of evidence from several sources.

their fierce looks, the clashing of their arms and the brandishing of their arms do us? These are mere symbols of barbarian boastfulness.'

Head taking

Another Celtic custom, only very briefly mentioned by Polybius, was the decapitation of their enemies. 'The consul Gaius fell fighting desperately in the thick of battle, and his head was brought to the Celtic king.' After a battle between the Senones and the Romans the consul got no news of the disaster 'till some Gallic horsemen came in sight with heads hanging from their horses' breasts or fixed on spears and singing their song of triumph as is their custom'. On another occasion the Boii killed a Roman leader, cut off his head and bore it off to their most holy temple. Then the skull was gilded and used as a sacred vessel for libations or as a drinking cup by the priest and temple attendants. During the Punic War, a Celtic contingent in the Roman army, believing that Hannibal's prospects were brighter, killed some Romans and, cutting off their heads, departed with them to join the Carthaginian.

'When their enemies fall', writes Diodorus Siculus, 'they [the Gauls] cut off their heads and fasten them to the necks of their horses. They hand over the blood-stained spoils to their attendants and they carry them off as booty chanting a paean over them and singing a hymn of victory. They nail up the heads on their houses just as certain hunters do when they have killed wild beasts. They embalm in cedar oil the heads of their most distinguished enemies and keep them carefully in a chest: they display them with pride to strangers, declaring that one of their ancestors or their father or the man himself refused to accept a large sum of money offered for this head. They say that some of them boast that they refused the weight of the head in gold.' Strabo repeats these details almost verbatim and claims that Posidonius had seen such heads displayed in many places and had at first been disgusted by the sight but later got used to it.

This head taking and the preservation of the heads of the most distinguished enemies was a practice which had for the Gauls a religious and a magical significance. To the Romans, however, it was a sure sign of inhuman savagery, and Strabo says the Romans put an end to it. Caesar does not mention the custom, and it may have died out by the time he started his campaigns in Gaul.

Chariots

In the early encounters of the Celts and the Romans, it was the war chariot which most attracted the Roman interest. It appears that the main use of the chariot was for causing panic when the charioteers drove against the enemy lines at top speed, throwing javelins and by mere speed and noise terrifying the enemy. 'Many of the first line were trodden underfoot by the rush of horses and chariots.' Once the initial stage of terrifying was over, the warriors dismounted from the chariots and fought on foot, while their attendants kept the chariot at the ready to effect, if necessary, a speedy retreat. The chariots were then merely a means of transport for the warriors to and from their combats, as in Homeric Greece. A thousand chariots took part in the battle of Sentinum (295 BC), and at Telamon (225 BC) the chariots were stationed on the wings.

'When going into battle,' says Diodorus Siculus, 'the Gauls use two-horsed chariots which carry the charioteer and the warrior. When they meet with cavalry in war, they throw their javelins at the enemy and, dismounting from their chariots, they join battle with their swords . . . They bring also freemen as servants, choosing them from among the poor, and these they use as charioteers and shield bearers'.

As their prowess and agility as horsemen increased, so the Gauls gradually gave up the chariot. Chariots were no longer in fashion when Caesar was conquering Gaul, and he was surprised to find them still in use in Britain. Strabo states that the Britons used chariots as did some of the Gauls, while Diodorus Siculus says that 'they used chariots as the heroes of Greece are traditionally said to have done in the Trojan War'.

Caesar's description of the Britons in action gives a good picture of their skill and agility. 'At first they ride along the whole line and hurl javelins; the terror inspired by the horses and the noise of the wheels generally throw the enemy ranks into confusion. Then when they have worked their way between the lines of their own cavalry, they jump down from the chariots and fight on foot. Meanwhile the drivers withdraw a little from the field and place the chariots so that their masters, if hard pressed by the enemy, have an easy retreat to their ranks . . . Their daily training and practice have made them so expert that they can control their horses at full gallop on a steep incline and then check and turn them in a moment. They can run along the chariot pole, stand on the yoke and return again into the chariot very speedily'.

The archaeological evidence for chariots comprises the metal pieces of the vehicle and the harness found in graves or in votive deposits. Representations on sculpture and on coins help to provide information about the wooden or wicker pieces that no longer survive. Harness was richly decorated with bronze ornaments, sometimes inlaid with coral or enamel. The leather does not survive, but the metal parts have been frequently found in burials and in hoards. Bridle bits, or snaffles, often consisted of three main elements: a central bar, sometimes itself jointed, with rings at each end by which the side loops or cheek pieces were attached to the reins. The leather harness was further elaborated at the strap junctions with a series of mountings of a variety of shapes and decoration. In order to allow the charioteer greater control of the horses, the reins were led over the wooden yoke through a series of bronze rings. Such rein rings (or terrets) were often decorated, but the wear marks where the reins strained the bronze show that they had a practical function. Several important deposits of metalwork of this type have been found in Britain, notably from Llyn Cerrig Bach (Anglesey, Gwynedd)(now in the National Museum of Wales), from Melsonby (North Yorkshire) and from Bawdrip (Somerset) (now in the British Museum).

The technology available to the Celtic wheelwright was the result of the experimentation and knowledge of many earlier generations of European craftsmen. On the continent the wooden rim was usually from a single piece of wood, or felloe, bent to a circular shape with the tapering ends brought together in a long overlapping scarf joint. This was kept in a position by a U-shaped iron clamp, thus keeping the hub and spokes together. The wheel was further strengthened by an iron tyre. A wheel of Celtic type, found in a rubbish pit on the Roman fort at Bar Hill (Dunbartonshire, Strathclyde), had survived because of the damp conditions; the felloe was a single piece of ash, the eleven spokes were of lathe-turned willow and the similarly turned hub was of elm. This careful choice of material shows the craftsman's appreciation of the qualities of the different woods. The iron tyre had been made in one piece and had been set round the felloe when still hot and then shrunk on to it, thus compressing the wood as it cooled. In Britain the more usual type of wheel has several sections to the felloe cut from a plank and joined by tenons; a wheel of second century BC date from Holme Pierrepont (Nottinghamshire) has six sections, with two of the twelve spokes in each, kept rigid by an iron tyre, which has been shrunk round the wooden frame.

The wheels were attached to the axle of a chariot by means of linchpins, often of iron with bronze decoration. Above the axle was the platform, probably about 1 metre (3 feet 3 inches) square, on which the warrior and charioteer stood, while at right angles to the axle the chariot pole rose from axle height about 0.5 metres 1 foot 8 inches) to the height of the shoulders of the horses, about 1.15 metres (3 feet 9 inches). There was probably considerable variation in the style of the sides of the platform, although lightness would have been important for speed. The use of wickerwork is mentioned in the Irish tales, and Fox favoured semicircular sides filled in with wicker, as shown in the reconstruction on fig. 13. However, a double arcade seems a better interpretation of the coin evidence, and there is an attractive model of this type in the British Museum. The front and back would be open, and the view from the platform looking along the pole (fig. 15) is a telling reminder of the agility of the warriors described by Caesar.

Several classical authors assert that the Celts had 'scythed

Fig. 14. Reconstructed horse harness.

chariots', and this notion has caught popular imagination since 1902, when a statue of Boudica standing in such a chariot was erected on Westminster Bridge. No archaeological corroboration for such additions to the hub caps has been found in Europe, though it seems that chariots with some form of hub projections were found in eastern warfare in the second and third centuries BC.

Cavalry

In war the Celts were particularly formidable as horsemen, having a reputation for excellence in mounted warfare. When the chiefs and nobles gave up the use of war chariots, they fought on horseback, using the horse as a means of getting to and from the battle. Polybius tells that the Iberian and Celtic cavalry were not a squadron of horsemen fighting as a unit, but merely mounted warriors who, once they arrived at the battle area, dismounted and fought on foot. German horsemen had trained their horses to remain on the same spot so that they could return to them quickly in case of need. The Celtiberian horsemen had a similar manoeuvre. They had small pegs attached to the horse's reins.

Fig. 15. The view along the chariot pole.

These they fixed into the ground, so that the horses could not stray, until they came back and pulled out the pegs.

Livy, writing of the early migrations, says that the Gauls set out with large forces of infantry and cavalry. At Telamon there were twenty thousand either on horseback or on chariots. Writing of the year 213 BC, after the Roman campaigns in Spain, Livy remarks that the only fact worth recording was that until then the Romans had never had mercenaries in their camp but now they had the Celtiberians. Contingents of Gallic cavalry fought on the Roman and Carthaginian sides during Hannibal's campaigns, choosing the side where the prospects and pay were better. When the Gauls were finally conquered, it was the Gallic cavalry that the Romans recruited for their army.

Describing the Celtic invasion of Greece, Pausanias speaks of the *trimarcisia* (*marca* was the Celtic word for a horse, he says); this was a group of three horsemen, one of them a nobleman and the two others grooms. The grooms would stay behind the ranks, ready to supply their master with a fresh horse if his were wounded; one groom would take his place if he were injured or killed, and the other would take him back to camp if he were wounded. The simple idea behind this scheme, it seems, was to keep the initial number of horsemen complete.

In his campaign across the Rhine, Caesar discovered that the Germans thought it shameful to use saddles, and they dared to engage with any number of saddled horsemen, regardless of by how much they were outnumbered. Presumably the Celtic cavalry in Caesar's army did have saddles, but neither the Celts nor the Romans had knowledge of stirrups. A few spurs have, however, survived (see also fig. 11). At Avaricum, Vercingetorix himself took command of the cavalry and lightly armed infantry (who regularly fought amongst the cavalry) to set an ambush at a place where they expected the Romans would go to forage.

5
Celtic weapons

Diodorus Siculus has given us a comprehensive description of Celtic armour and weapons: 'For arms they have man-sized shields decorated in a manner peculiar to them. Some of these have projecting figures in bronze, skilfully wrought not only for decoration but also for protection. They wear bronze helmets with large projecting figures which give the wearer the appearance of enormous size. In some cases horns are attached so as to form one piece, in others the foreparts of birds or quadrupeds worked in relief. . . . Some of them have iron breastplates, wrought in chain, while others are satisfied with the arms Nature has given them and fight naked. Instead of the short sword they carry long swords held by a chain of iron or bronze and hanging along their right flank. Some of them have gold – or silver – plated belts round their tunics. They brandish spears which are called *lanciae* and which have iron heads a cubit in length and even more, and a little less than two palms in breadth: for their swords are not shorter than the spears of others, and the heads of their spears are longer than the swords of others. Some of these are forged straight, others are twisted and have a spiral form for their whole length, so that the blow may not only cut the flesh but also tear it in pieces and so that the withdrawal of the spear may lacerate the wound.'

Shields

Pausanias says that the Celts had no other defensive armour than their national shields and, according to Livy, their shields were oblong and long, commensurate with their bodies. One disadvantage of wooden shields was that they might be pierced, and, in some battles, it is reported that several shields were pierced by one spear and locked together. Again so many spears became stuck in the shields that they were too heavy to carry. Boudica, exhorting her troops before battle, scorned the Roman helmets, breastplates and greaves, saying that the Britons believed that their shields gave greater protection than did the whole suits of mail of the Romans.

The archaeological evidence for Celtic shields is widespread both from graves such as those mentioned in chapter 3 and from votive deposits, but because they were largely made from

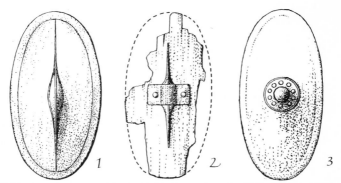

Fig 16. Celtic shields: 1, oval shield with binding strip and midrib; 2, oval shield with strip boss and midrib; 3, oval shield with round central boss.

perishable materials (wood, leather, wickerwork) it is most often the metal parts that alone survive—the iron boss at the centre of the shield, the occasional metal binding or hand grip (fig. 16). Thus we lack any sense of the decoration described by Diodorus and of the variety of applied designs that must have added to the individuality of the shields, except for the Witham shield, where there are traces of the figure of a boar that had been fixed to the front of the shield, and for the representations on the arch at Orange (fig. 17). Shields were often made up of several planks of wood forming long ovals or sometimes elongated hexagons in shape. Several wooden shields were thrown, as part of a ritual deposit, into the waters of the Lac de Neuchatel in Switzerland at a place known as La Tène. The shields measure about 1.1 metres (3 feet 7 inches) long and 0.6 metres (2 feet) broad at the middle and comprised three planks butted together. A central hole, which contained the hand grip, was covered by a hollowed wooden boss, which was itself kept in position by a strip of iron

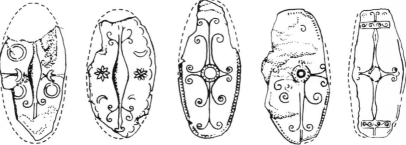

Fig. 17. Arc de Triomphe, Orange (Vaucluse, France); details of shields.

Fig. 18. Police riot shields of today are of similar size and used in a similar fashion to those of the Celts.

Fig. 19. Shield from the river Thames at Battersea, London; detail of the central boss. This elaborate piece is the bronze cover for a wooden or leather shield and is one of the most accomplished pieces of British Celtic art; it belongs to the first half of the first century AD.

Fig. 20. Distance slab commemorating the completion of part of the Antonine Wall, Bridgeness (West Lothian); this panel, which is to the side of the central inscription, shows defeated barbarians, sword, spears and shields with round bosses.

riveted on either side of the boss.

A line of warriors bearing brightly decorated shields must have been a frightening sight. To give an impression of the protection that they would have provided we illustrate the use of shields of not dissimilar size overlapping one with another—modern police riot shields (fig. 18). The shapes of the various parts that made up a shield altered over the centuries, and on the continent it is possible to group the various types of boss, for example, into chronological classes. In Britain several surviving shields are very much more elaborate than are continental examples, and these were perhaps parade pieces, diplomatic gifts or sumptuous objects with a religious significance. The central boss of the shield from the river Thames at Battersea is an example of such rich decoration (fig. 19).

Roman memorial stones in England and commemorative slabs on the Antonine Wall in Scotland illustrate several defeated Celts with their weapons lying beside them; in several cases particular attention has been given to the depiction of the distinctively Celtic hairstyle. Such grave slabs have been found at Chester, Hexham and Cirencester. At Wroxeter the naked warrior bears a sword and an oval shield with a long midrib. The slab from Bridgeness (West Lothian) shows defeated warriors with their swords, shields and spears (fig. 20). The shields presumably illustrate the type current in the mid second century AD in the north; they are shown as rectangular with round bosses. A wooden shield with its leather cover still surviving was found in Littleton Bog, Clonoura, County Tipperary, Ireland; the boss too is covered by leather (fig. 21).

Swords

The Celtic sword was good for a cut, says Polybius, but not for a thrust; he also implies that after the first cutting blow the edges became blunt and the blade so bent that unless the warrior had time to straighten the blade with his foot he could not deliver a second blow. The archaeological evidence shows, however, that some swordsmiths at least were producing weapons of a very high order, and indeed some are marked by the maker's own sign (fig. 22). Tacitus describes the British swords as long and unsuited to fighting in a confined space or at close quarters; here they could not swing their long swords. Dionysius of Halicarnassus describes how they raised their swords aloft and smote—throwing the whole weight of their bodies into the blows and delivering blows as if they intended to cut to pieces all that opposed them.

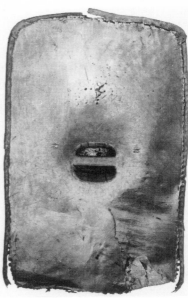

Fig. 21. Clonoura (County Tipperary, Ireland): both sides of a shield made of wooden planks covered with leather.
Fig. 22. Swords and scabbards from La Tène, Lac de Neuchatel (Switzerland), showing a maker's mark in the shape of a boar, and decoration at the mouth of a scabbard.

Fig. 23. Swords and scabbards from La Tène, Lac de Neuchatel (Switzerland).

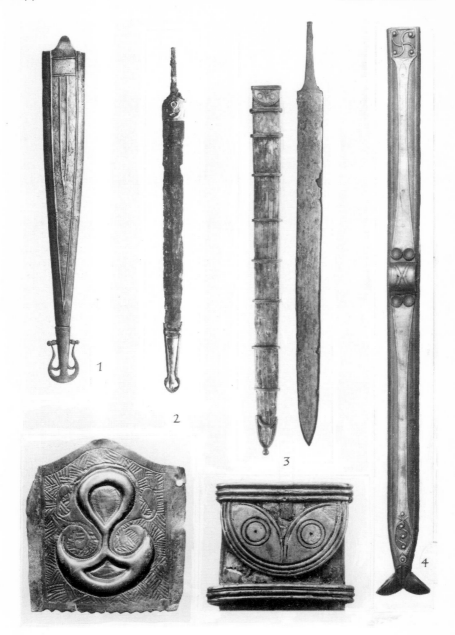

1

2

3

4

Several broad groups of swords and scabbards have been identified on the continent and in Britain, largely by the length of the sword and the decoration of the scabbard; although scabbards might be thought to provide limited opportunity for decoration, the mouth of the scabbard (that part where it was attached by a strap or chain to the sword belt) (fig. 23) and the tip (often strengthened by an additional binding or chape) offered considerable scope for the Celtic craftsman. In length the sword from La Gorge Meillet measured 0.74 metres (2 feet 5 inches). Later examples, like those illustrated with their respective scabbards from La Tène (fig. 23), are 0.66 metres (2 feet 2 inches) and 0.68 metres (2 feet 3 inches); Stead has shown from a detailed study that the earlier swords could be used for thrusting as well as cutting, while the later and often narrower swords were more suitable for slashing. The swords of the latest period of Celtic activity on the continent are longer and wider than such examples, with scabbards with rounded ends and often a laddered decoration. In Britain a wide variety of swords and scabbards has been found and four are illustrated to give an impression of the range (fig. 24); the wooden scabbard from Stanwick (North Yorkshire) is an important reminder of how much perishable material from this period has been lost.

Spears

There were two kinds of spear, the broad-bladed spear for thrusting, and the lighter spear or javelin for throwing. Strabo says the Celts carried 'a long shield and spears of like size and the *madaris*, which is a kind of javelin. The Germans carried spears called in their language *frameae* with short narrow blades, but so sharp and easy to handle that they were equally useful in fighting at close quarters or at a distance.' Many spearheads and javelin heads survive in a multitude of shapes and sizes, varying from 500 millimetres (19¾ inches) to 100 millimetres (4 inches) often with traces of their ash shafts in their sockets (fig. 25). Two complete spears were discovered at La Tène, both nearly 2.5 metres (8 feet 2 inches) long. Spear butts, which were designed to improve the balance of the weapon, have been discovered in many burials.

Fig. 24. Swords and scabbards from Britain: 1, dagger scabbard from Minster Ditch (Oxfordshire), one of the earliest pieces of British Celtic art, dating to about 300 BC; 2, sword and scabbard decoration, Standlake (Oxfordshire); 3, scabbard and sword, Stanwick (North Yorkshire); 4, scabbard, Mortonhall, Edinburgh. Various scales.

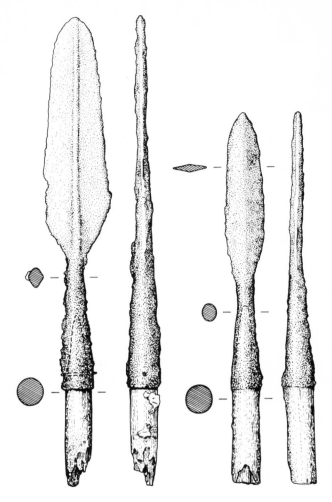

Fig. 25. Spearheads from a burial at Camelon (Stirlingshire, Central Region).

Helmets

Except among the Italian tribes perhaps, Celtic helmets were comparatively rare, but several are of great magnificence. The helmet from La Gorge Meillet has already been mentioned; it is impressive but impractical. In fourth-century Italy cast bronze helmets with top-knobs, known as 'jockey caps', were fashionable, some of which had cheek pieces. A unique find from a burial at Ciumeşti in Romania has a helmet which is surmounted by a bronze bird with wings hinged to the body to allow them to flap (fig. 26). This must have been an awesome sight and may be compared with the representation on the Gundestrup Cauldron (fig. 11). The addition of horns, mentioned by Diodorus, has appeared in many reconstructions of Celtic warriors, but the evidence for them is slight; they are shown on the arch at Orange and on the Gundestrup Cauldron, but they are not common as representations. Even the most famous helmet, that from the river Thames at Waterloo Bridge, was almost certainly created as a votive deposit rather than mirroring a more practical example,

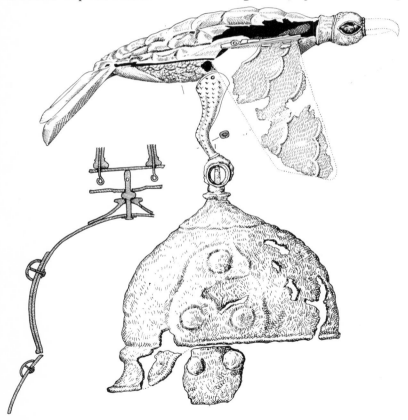

Fig. 26. Helmet surmounted by a bird with hinged wings, Ciumeşti (Romania).

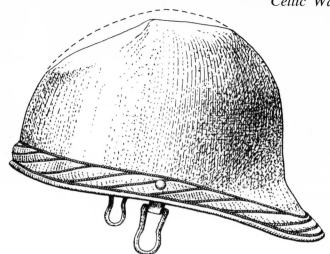

Fig. 27. Helmet from the river Rhine at Mainz (Germany).

like that from the Rhine at Mainz (fig. 27). The flamboyant repoussé decoration on the neck guard of a helmet in the British Museum is complemented by studs which would have been infilled with red enamel (fig. 28). The sense of grim military reality of the later stages of Celtic warfare is demonstrated by a helmet from a grave at Giubiasco (Ticino, Switzerland), a sturdy iron bowl with neck guard and cheek pieces (fig. 29).

Mail

The use of body armour among the Celtic tribes is confirmed by a small number of archaeological finds and representations, and it is probable that the invention of linked metal rings to form mail was made in a Celtic armoury. We illustrate a fragment of mail with an elaborate bronze stud from the burial at Ciumeşti in Romania (fig. 30). Two methods of manufacture were found in the mail from this burial: in one alternating rows of punched-out rings with loops merely butted together (like bath-plug chains), while, instead of these, the second method employed rings that were riveted together. There are several fleeting references to more complete breastplates, but these must have been very rare indeed. Marcellus is said to have pierced the breastplate of his Celtic adversary with his lance, and Marius was faced at Vercellae by Cimbri who were reported to be wearing breastplates. Vettius Bolanus, governor of Britain (69-71 AD), took a breastplate from a British king to form part of a trophy.

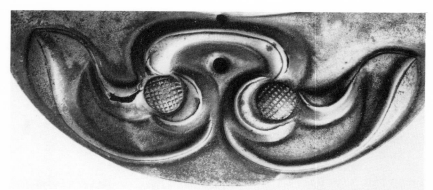

Fig. 28. Helmet without known find spot, now in the British Museum: detail of neckguard.

Fig. 29. Helmet from Giubiasco (Ticino, Switzerland).

Archery and slings

Some Celts use bows and slings, says Strabo, and in the context of human sacrifices 'they used to shoot men down with arrows'. In his war against Caesar, Vercingetorix ordered all the archers who could be found (and there was a very large number in Gaul) to be sent to him; in this way he made good his losses at Avaricum. The Gauls, according to Caesar's report, placed archers and light-armed infantry among the calvary to support them if they had to retreat, and on another front they used slings to hurl moulded balls of red-hot clay and incendiary darts.

There is little archaeological evidence for the use of archery in warfare, but iron arrowheads of triangular tanged form have been found on a number of sites and have been studied particularly at Alésia (Côte-d'Or). Slings themselves do not survive, being made of leather, but their importance may be shown in two ways: firstly in the shape of hillfort defences in the first century BC in southern Britain, and secondly in the huge hoards of sling stones that were prepared in readiness for sudden attack. The depth of the defences at Maiden Castle (Dorset) or Danebury (Hampshire) may be related to an increase in the use of the sling in warfare, and Cunliffe has suggested that the complex east entrance at Danebury could have been effectively supervised by slingers on the central hornwork covering a radius of up to 60 metres (65 yards). At Maiden Castle one hoard of 22,260 stones had been prepared beside the eastern gateway; the majority were beach pebbles of approximately 50 grams (1¾ ounces), but some were specially prepared in clay. Such a hoard is, as Wheeler remarked, 'a vivid token of deliberate and orderly preparation and of civic discipline'.

Celts in perspective

We have tried to give an impression both of one aspect of Celtic society and of the different types of evidence that may be used to build up this picture. But no single picture of the Celtic warrior is possible, for we are viewing a period of five centuries over a wide geographical canvas and with the warriors responding to very different social and political pressures. With the burial of La Gorge Meillet or the stories of single combat and ritually naked warriors, we sense a golden age of a society creating its own pressures and perhaps its own myths; with the decapitated and dejected warriors of the Bridgeness slab we see a society in military defeat. Different weapons and battle strategies were appropriate when the pressure of Rome became increasingly

Fig. 30. Mail fragment from a burial at Ciumeşti (Romania).

intense, as the pages of Caesar's *Gallic Wars* show. While we need not, indeed must not, believe all that we read from classical sources, they give, in conjunction with the archaeological evidence, a unique flavour to our understanding of the warrior tribes at a time when much of Europe was moving from prehistory into history.

6
Museums

Several museums in Britain contain unrivalled collections of objects which help to evoke Celtic warfare and weapons. Most important is the **British Museum,** Great Russell Street, London WC1B 3DG (Telephone: 01-636 1555/8), with extensive displays of continental material as well as many of the most impressive pieces of highly ornamented weapons, perhaps originally for parade or display. There are several practical shield bosses, which are mounted on replica shields, as well as the intricate Battersea and Witham shields. The hoards from Melsonby (Stanwick) and Bawdrip (Polden Hills) have many beautifully decorated pieces of horse gear. Swords from La Tène, as well as many British finds, including Stanwick with its scabbard, are displayed.

The **National Museum of Wales,** Cathays Park, Cardiff CF1 3NP (Telephone: Cardiff [0222] 397951), has a fine collection of shield mountings. The **National Museum of Antiquities of Scotland,** Queen Street, Edinburgh, EH2 1JD (Telephone: 031-556 3550), has a remarkable collection including the Deskford carnyx (fig. 10) and the chariot model shown in figs. 13-15. Another chariot model is on display in the **Vindolanda Museum,** (The Vindolanda Trust), Bardon Mill, Hexham, Northumberland NE47 7JN (Telephone: Bardon Mill [049 84] 277). Many of the most important finds from Humberside are in the **Kingston upon Hull Transport and Archaeology Museum,** 36 High Street, Hull, North Humberside HU1 1NQ (Telephone: Hull [0482] 222737), including the chariot burial from Garton Slack (fig. 8). The Whitcombe burial is beautifully reconstructed in the **Dorset County Museum,** High West Street, Dorchester, Dorset DT1 1XA (Telephone: Dorchester [0305] 62735), whilst the Owslebury burial may be seen in the **Winchester City Museum,** The Square, Winchester, Hampshire SO23 9ES (Telephone: Winchester [0962] 68166).

7
Further reading

Brailsford, J. *Early Celtic Masterpieces from Britain in the British Museum.* British Museum. 1975.

Brewster, T. C. M. 'The Garton Slack chariot burial, East Yorkshire.' *Antiquity,* 45 (1971), 289-92.

Connolly, P. *Hannibal and the Enemies of Rome.* Macdonald. 1978.

Cunliffe, B. *Iron Age Communities in Britain.* Routledge and Kegan Paul. 1974.

Cunliffe, B. *Danebury: Anatomy of an Iron Age Hillfort.* Batsford. 1983.

Filip, J. *Celtic Civilisation and its Heritage.* Czechoslovak Academy of Sciences. English edition 1962.

Fox, Sir C. *A Find of the Early Iron Age from Llyn Cerrig Bach, Anglesey.* National Museum of Wales. 1946.

Harding, D. W. *The Iron Age in Lowland Britain.* Routledge and Kegan Paul. 1974.

Harding, D. W. *Prehistoric Europe.* Elsevier-Phaidon. 1978.

Jackson, K. H. *The Oldest Irish Tradition: A Window on the Iron Age.* Cambridge University Press. 1964.

McMahon, A. (editor). *The Celtic Way of Life.* Dublin Education Authority. 1976.

Megaw, J. V. S. *Art of the European Iron Age. A Study of the Elusive Image.* Adams and Dart. 1970.

Nash, D. 'Reconstructing Poseidonios' Celtic Ethnography: some considerations.' *Britannia,* 7 (1976), 111-26.

Piggott, S. *Ancient Europe from the beginnings of Agriculture to Classical Antiquity.* Edinburgh University Press. 1965.

Piggott, S. *The Earliest Wheeled Transport. From the Atlantic Coast to the Caspian Sea.* Thames and Hudson. 1983.

Powell, T. G. E. *The Celts.* Thames and Hudson. 1983.

Ross, A. *Everyday Life of the Pagan Celts.* Batsford. 1970.

Savory, H. N. *Guide Catalogue of the Early Iron Age Collections.* National Museum of Wales. 1976.

Stead, I. M. 'La Tène Swords and Scabbards in Champagne.' *Germania,* 61, ii (1983), 487-510.

Stead, I. M. *The Arras Culture.* Yorkshire Philosphical Society. 1979.

Stead, I. M. *The Gauls. Celtic Antiquities from France.* British Museum. 1981.

Tierney, J. J. 'The Celtic Ethnography of Posidonius.' *Proc. Royal Irish Academy,* 60 C (1960), 189-275.

The classical authors who describe Celtic warriors at length are the following:

Polybius. *Histories,* ii, chapters 14-31 (Greek).

Diodorus Siculus. *History,* v, chapters 25-32 (Greek).

Strabo. *Geography,* iv, chapters 1-4 (Greek).

Caesar. *De Bello Gallico,* vi, chapters 11-28 (Latin). Expeditions to Britain, iv, 20-36; v, 8-23.

Tacitus. *Agricola* (Latin).

Athenaeus. *Deipnosophistae,* iv, chapters 34, 36, 37, 40, 49 (Greek).

Pausanias. *Guide to Greece,* x, 19-23 (Greek).

All of these are found with translations in the Loeb Editions, and some in the Penguin Classics.

Index